Panoramic Ohio

PHOTOGRAPHS BY THOMAS R. SCHIFF

Panoramic Ohio

Cincinnati Art Museum

Copyright ©2002 by the Cincinnati Art Museum

All rights reserved. No part of this publication
may be reproduced without written permission of the
Cincinnati Art Museum.

Published in conjunction with the exhibition organized by the
Cincinnati Art Museum, Cincinnati, Ohio, February 2 to April 27, 2003.

PHOTOGRAPHY: Thomas R. Schiff
INTRODUCTION BY: Dennis Kiel
PHOTOGRAPH DESCRIPTIONS BY: Felix Winternitz
DIGITAL IMAGE MANIPULATION: Jacob Drabik
GRAPHIC DESIGN: Paul Neff Design, Cincinnati, Ohio
EDITED BY: John Fox
PHOTO OF THOMAS R. SCHIFF BY: Jymi Bolden

Library of Congress Cataloging-in-Publication Data

Schiff, Thomas R.
　Panoramic Ohio : photographs / by Thomas R. Schiff.
　　p. cm.
　Includes index.
　ISBN 0-931537-26-6 (hardcover edition) — ISBN 0-931537-25-8 (softcover edition)
　1. Ohio—Pictorial works. 2. Ohio—Description and travel. I. Title.
　F492 .S35 2002
　977.1'043'0222—dc21

　　　　　　　　　　　2002004079

Manufactured in China

Panoramic Ohio

Photographs by Thomas R. Schiff

Cincinnati Art Museum, Cincinnati, Ohio

This page and on the cover: BICENTENNIAL BARN, MOUNT VERNON

Acknowledgements

In more ways than one, Panoramic Ohio was a long journey from first photograph to finished book. I spent countless hours driving the length and breadth of the state, often just me, my camera and my car — looking for the right angle, waiting for the right sunlight, seeking the right event to document.

That was the easy part. Photography is my passion, after all, and there are few places I'd rather be than behind a camera.

Making a book, well, that's another story. It was a real team effort that took a lot of work from a lot of people. I'd like to personally thank:

Steve George, executive director of the Ohio Bicentennial Commission, who graciously included this project in the official celebration of the state's Bicentennial

Timothy Rub, director of the Cincinnati Art Museum, **Dennis Kiel**, associate curator of photography at the Cincinnati Art Museum, and **Sarah Sedlacek**, publication and web site coordinator at the Cincinnati Art Museum, who facilitated the printing of this book and who organized a companion exhibition of my panoramic photos

Paul Neff of Paul Neff Design, whose creative vision over the years has elevated my panoramic photos to a new level

Felix Winternitz, Cincinnati-based freelance writer, who researched and wrote the extended photo descriptions

About the Panoramic Photographs

The photographs in *Panoramic Ohio* were made from 1996 to 2002. The angle of view varies from 180 to 400 degrees, with most photos showing approximately a 300 degree view.

All photos were taken with the Hulcherama 360 Panoramic Camera, manufactured by Charles A. Hulcher Co., Hampton, Virginia. The camera sets up on a tripod and rotates automatically for a 360 degree picture, or it can be operated manually for shorter rotations. The rate of rotation varies from 2 seconds for a higher speed turn to 64 seconds for a low-speed turn.

John Fox, editor of *Cincinnati CityBeat*, for his editing skills throughout the book

Jonathan Valin, renowned Cincinnati author, for his advice on this and my previous panoramic photography projects

Jacob Drabik, graphic designer and Photoshop expert, for his tireless attention to detail

Barry Andersen, professor of photography at Northern Kentucky University, who helped create a whole new visual reality with the magic of computers

Jeffrey Siereveld of Mad Macs, for his digital scans from photo negatives

Mark Doyle of Autumn Color and **Scott Belmer** of Robin Imaging for their up-to-the-minute digital technology

Richard Hill of Charles A. Hulcher Co., manufacturer of my odd camera-of-choice

I also thank all those folks at organizations, events and institutions around Ohio who humored me by helping arrange these photographs. I hope it was worth their trouble.

Thomas R. Schiff

Dear Fellow Ohioans:

Like so many individuals, families, communities and institutions, Tom Schiff and the Cincinnati Art Museum have accepted the challenge of the Ohio Bicentennial to undertake their own very special project to help Ohio celebrate its 200th birthday. Following his magnificent collection of panoramic photographs of the Cincinnati area, Tom has now captured a portrait of Ohio on the eve of its Bicentennial.

This splendid collection of truly extraordinary photographs allows each of us to see our state as it has never been seen before. Moreover, Tom has brought diversity of landscape, ethnicity, culture and character of our decentralized state. One hundred years from now, when Ohioans prepare for the state's Tricentennial, Tom's panoramic images will provide them with a unique view of the Ohio we know and love.

Likewise, the Cincinnati Art Museum, by organizing a traveling exhibition of Tom's Ohio images, is contributing meaningfully to the Bicentennial and its spirit of education and creativity. Together, this beautiful book and its companion exhibition will help all of us learn more about, and celebrate, Ohio.

Congratulations to both Tom Schiff and the Cincinnati Art Museum for an outstanding Bicentennial project!

Sincerely,

Bob Taft

Governor of Ohio

Cities and Towns Photographed

1. Celina
2. Wapakoneta
3. Columbus Grove
4. Toledo
5. Bowling Green
6. Tiffin
7. Upper Sandusky
8. Bucyrus
9. Mansfield
10. Milan
11. Oberlin
12. Cleveland
13. Kirtland
14. Akron
15. Lisbon
16. Youngstown
17. East Liverpool
18. Wooster
19. Mount Vernon
20. Newark
21. Athens
22. Zanesville
23. Millersburg
24. Coshocton
25. Somerset
26. Columbus
27. Clifton
28. Dayton
29. Cincinnati
30. Laurelville
31. Hamilton
32. Coalton
33. Chillicothe
34. McConnelsville
35. Logan
36. Gallipolis

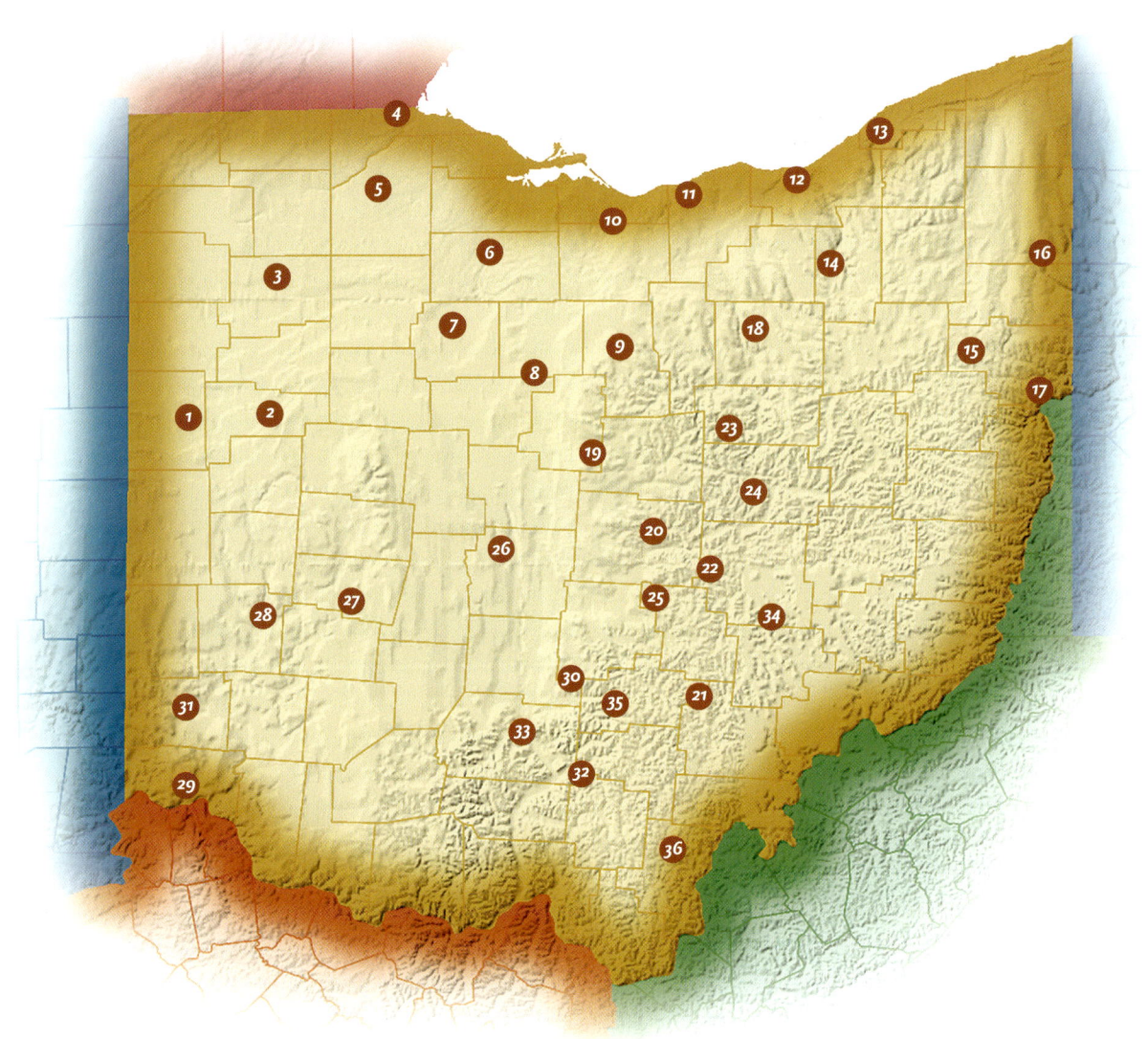

Introduction

For almost thirty years, Tom Schiff has devoted much of his life to photography. The path his "visual journey" has taken, with its several twists and turns, makes for a fascinating study. At first glance, his work could be divided into two distinct and well-defined categories. In the beginning, Tom created beautifully crafted, black-and-white prints shot with a 4x5 or 8x10 inch (which refers to the size of the negatives produced) view camera. He often focused on subject matter found in urban areas: architectural details and storefront facades and windows. Reviewing these images, one can see a serious interest in light, form and texture.

This early body of work appears to be in stark contrast with his most recent photographs, the colorful and visually complex 360 degree panoramic images found in this catalogue. Tom has spent the last eight or nine years literally photographing the world around him, catching all sides of a scene, and making visible on paper what is basically impossible to see at one time in real life. It is quite possible to say Tom has gone from shooting the "natural" world to one that might be defined as "unnatural" or, in some respects, "unreal."

It is understandable why his panoramic photographs are often discussed as a separate entity. But are they really that different from his black-and-white prints? Is it possible to find a similar theme or common thread throughout his work to unify his entire career?

Tom's basic theme has always been ordinary subject matter — objects or scenes one might observe every day but in the end take for granted. These might include a mysterious form reflected on a window, an abstract shape found on the side of a deteriorating building, or the bright, flowing patterns constructed from the interior of a diner. In any case, Tom's ultimate goal is the same: to make us stop and look at things and, for that matter, the world around us, in a very different manner.

Born in Cincinnati, Tom Schiff took his first photographs with a Kodak Brownie camera when he was a young boy. Not long afterwards, he began making contact prints in a small darkroom that he set up in a coal bin in the basement of his parents' house. It was in high school, when Tom was working as a photographer for the school newspaper, that he saw a book of Ansel Adams' photographs and was immediately impressed by the quality of the prints. Adams became a major influence as did Minor White, whose work Tom studied after entering college. He was fascinated with the abstract aspects of White's compositions, as well as his personal sense of vision — the very qualities that Tom had hoped to achieve during his own photographic career.

Tom pursued a career in business at Ohio University in Athens, Ohio, but he also enrolled in a number of courses in photography and art history, studying with Clarence White, Jr. and Arnold Gasson, among others. He used the camera sporadically after college but found new inspiration after several photography outings with his friend, Paul Schrantz. Beginning in the 1970s and throughout the 1980s, Tom's black-and-white prints were shown in exhibitions throughout the country, and many found their way into the permanent collections of the New Orleans Museum of Art, the Milwaukee Center for Photography, the Baltimore Museum of Art and the Cincinnati Art Museum.

© Thomas R. Schiff, *Barbershop, Detroit*, 1981, gelatin silver print, Cincinnati Art Museum, Museum purchase: Gift of Amy Bubenhofer, by exchange, 1985.262

Tom's interest in photography has extended beyond the role of working photographer. In the early 1980s, he became a founding member of Images Center for Photography, a gallery and professional organization for photography enthusiasts, located in Cincinnati. He also produced PhotoProfiles, a series of informative documentary videos on major living photographers.

By the early 1990s, however, Tom saw his work becoming static and repetitious. Looking for a new creative outlet, he began shooting panoramic photographs, an area he had investigated briefly in the mid-1980s. With the ability to photograph up to, and well beyond, 360 degrees, Tom has managed to take the panoramic image to an extreme level.

In one sense, Tom's panoramic photographs have become a natural extension of what appears to be his ultimate goal: to convince us to appreciate the beauty of things that surround us everyday. When asked to describe his photographs in *Panoramic Ohio*, Tom has often used the words "illusion," "multiple images" and "reflection" — elements that can be found in his early work as well. Sifting through it all, one might ultimately discover that there is a single focus — and with Tom behind the lens, a variety of approaches to get there.

— *Dennis Kiel, Associate Curator of Photography, Cincinnati Art Museum*

Amphicar Swim In, Celina

There's only one Ohio festival where you can expect to hear much tech talk about the physics of aquaplaning and such odd expressions as "dipping the headlights." And that would be the annual Amphicar Owners Club Swim In, which takes place each summer in Celina. Some 40 to 50 of these peculiar amphibious vehicles drive in — or dive in — for the event. There's both a street parade on wheels and a floating parade where the Amphicars coast single file under a one-lane bridge that leads to the lake.

The Amphicar was manufactured in Berlin (Germany, not Ohio) from 1962 to 1967; only 3,000 were ever produced, with about 500 remaining worldwide. It's the only nonmilitary amphibious vehicle ever made on an automobile production line, with glorious rear fins rising higher than any American classic car ever conceived. The watertight steel craft can sail along the highway at 70 miles per hour (or at 8 knots on the water).

How did the Swim In land in Celina after many years in New York? There's chatter in official club literature that claims Celina was determined the "actual exact and true navigational center" of the club membership. (That would be 40.5555 degrees North latitude by 84.6061 degrees West longitude, for those of you contemplating a voyage there.)

But Amphicar fans concede that the benefits offered by the city sealed the deal, including free meeting halls, complimentary use of the city helicopter, free police escorts and no-cost use of boat ramps that access Grand Lake St. Mary's.

MERCER COUNTY FAIR, CELINA

Wapa Theatre, Wapakoneta

Swimming Pool, Columbus Grove

SWIMMING POOL, COLUMBUS GROVE

Toledo Art Museum, Toledo

TOLEDO ART MUSEUM, TOLEDO

glass city 200, Toledo Speedway, Toledo

GLASS CITY 200, TOLEDO SPEEDWAY, TOLEDO

B-29 Cockpit, Toledo

B-29 COCKPIT, TOLEDO

15

Wood County Courthouse, Bowling Green

The majestic county courthouse in downtown Bowling Green is a tribute to the Romanesque style of architecture, constructed in 1896 for the then outrageous sum of $255,746.84. Temporary railroad tracks had to be installed leading up to the building site so that the 750 train carloads of sandstone, limestone, marble and granite could be delivered.

Among the unique aspects of this structure are stained glass, sculpture of animals (such as snakes representing vice and corruption) and a square clock tower that stands an imposing 190 feet tall. The hands on the clock extend to a diameter of 16 feet, at one time the largest in America with the exception of the 17-foot dials on the *San Francisco Chronicle* building. Accuracy isn't a hallmark of the timepiece, however — a local editorial at the time reported the clock "goes when it pleases and makes its own time." The clock has frozen stiff just once, in the Blizzard of 1978.

Bowling Green, a town of approximately 30,000 residents, is the county seat and home to Bowling Green State University. The courthouse isn't the town's only unique architectural landmark — nearby is a 45-foot-high windmill constructed by a Dutch builder to mask an unsightly smokestack.

Uncle Mike's Ice Cream, Tiffin

18

UNCLE MIKE'S ICE CREAM, TIFFIN

Music at the Mural, Bucyrus

When artist Eric Grohe began painting his massive mural in the heart of Bucyrus, drivers pulled over their cars at the village square to stop and talk. In fact, it was those very discussions that inspired Grohe to name his mural *Great American Crossroads*.

You see, the $70,000 mural — depicting life in old Bucyrus circa 1890 to 1915 — was created at the intersection of state routes 30 and 4. So the curious drivers were traveling along either 30 (the old Lincoln Highway that runs from California to New York) or 4 (which runs from Tallahassee, Florida, all the way to the shores of Lake Erie) — essentially, citizens from all across America would stop to watch Grohe paint the 34-by-130-foot tapestry. He used Sherwin Williams house paint, if you're wondering.

"The people in the mural are real, people like Harvey Firestone and Henry Ford, so it's like a huge history lesson about the time when the horse and buggy gave way to the automobile," observes Deb Pinion, director of the Bucyrus Chamber of Commerce, which commissioned the artwork. Bucyrus, a town of 13,000, is primarily a manufacturing center and is still the only producer of copper kettles in the United States and the country's largest garden hose manufacturer.

Each summer, the Bucyrus chamber sponsors Music at the Mural, a concert series at the park where the artwork is located. On any given week, big band, rock, country and Christian music is featured.

Town Square, Mansfield

TOWN SQUARE, MANSFIELD

Melon Festival Parade, Milan

MELON FESTIVAL PARADE, MILAN

Graduation, Oberlin

24

GRADUATION, OBERLIN

church in snow, Cleveland

CHURCH IN SNOW, CLEVELAND

Skyline, Sunrise, Cleveland

PUBLIC SQUARE, SUNSET, CLEVELAND

Hall of Fame and Science Center, Cleveland

The first four words visitors often utter when entering the gleaming Rock and Roll Hall of Fame are, "Why here? Why Cleveland?"

A reasonable question. Turns out that Cleveland disc jockey Alan Freed, who is credited with coining the term "rock and roll," practically invented the genre. Well, maybe not invented, but certainly promoted the heck out of it as a WJW radio personality, playing "R&B uptempo" (as it was known then) as early as 1951.

Today, the Rock Hall (on right and left of photograph in the foreground) stands on Cleveland's lakefront shore, a monument to Freed and his musical generation. Each year, the hall inducts a half-dozen bands, songwriters and performers (including the likes of Talking Heads, Isaac Hayes, The Ramones and Brenda Lee) as curators slowly amass a cross-section of rock and roll history.

Just down the banks of Lake Erie stands the Great Lakes Science Center (center of photograph), a wildly popular nonprofit educational institution focusing on scientific, environmental and technological activities in the Great Lakes region. People love its "hands on, minds on" exhibits, educational programming and OMNIMAX Theater.

Along with the new Cleveland Browns football stadium, the Rock Hall and the Science Center have helped transformed the city's lakefront.

The Flats, Cleveland

THE FLATS, CLEVELAND

Westside Market, Cleveland

WESTSIDE MARKET, CLEVELAND

Library, Cleveland

Severance Hall, Cleveland

Holden Arboretum, Kirtland

HOLDEN ARBORETUM, KIRTLAND

English Garden, Stan Hywet Hall and Gardens, Akron

Akron Aeros at Canal Park Stadium, Akron

AKRON AEROS AT CANAL PARK STADIUM, AKRON

SOAP BOX DERBY, AKRON

Steel Trolley Diner, Lisbon

Travel along the old Lincoln Highway (now Route 30) into the bucolic hamlet of Lisbon, and you'll come to what has become something of an institution in these parts: Earle and Jacki's Steel Trolley Diner.

Diner aficionados from across the Midwest converge on this vintage culinary and chrome attraction, which is most definitely a diner — although its pedigree as a trolley is somewhat in question. The proprietors at this 1956 O'Mahony classic diner are, not surprisingly, Earle and Jacki. A clock overhead stipulates "Time To Eat Good Food," and that's no idle boast; the restaurant routinely wins awards and media attention, including a recent *Ohio Magazine* story on "Picture Perfect Pies." (The pie in question, if you're wondering, is the diner's fresh apple crumb.)

At the Steel Trolley Diner, the coffee's strong, the neon's a vibrant pink and there's usually a stool at the luncheon counter or a booth available. Sniff the scent of fresh-cut French fries, nab a slice of the oatmeal or apple pie and relish the sounds coming out of the jukebox, which is crammed with 1950s rock & roll. (Earle tossed out the cigarette machine to make way for this musical majesty.)

"Come visit us any time," says Earle. "We're open pretty much every hour of the day and night." And, yes, the waitresses may well call you "Hon."

Town Square, Lisbon

Fellows Riverside Gardens, Youngstown

FELLOWS RIVERSIDE GARDENS, YOUNGSTOWN

41

Diamond Area, East Liverpool

DIAMOND AREA, EAST LIVERPOOL

Air Force Band Concert, Wooster

Waco Airplane Reunion, Mt Vernon

If you overhear somebody chatting about Wacos or "flying the Koop," you've undoubtedly run across some barnstorming enthusiast or a daring biplane pilot. These folks flock each summer to Wynkoop Airport in Mount Vernon, home to the Annual Waco Aircraft Reunion and Fly-In.

It's all thanks to the Waco Aircraft Company, which first opened for business in the early 1920s to capitalize on the daredevil pilot exhibitions then sweeping the country. The manufacturer was founded in Lorain by Elwood "Sam" Junkin and Clayton Bruckner along with a well-known barnstormer of the era, Buck Weaver (thus the moniker Waco, short for Weaver Airplane Company).

The biplanes were specially designed and reinforced to endure the aerial histrionics and loopy loops favored by the crazed pilots of the day. By 1929, the firm had evolved into the most prolific producer of light aircraft in the nation.

Today, a few bold enthusiasts keep the legacy of the original Waco biplanes alive. A trip to Mount Vernon and Wynkoop Airport for the Reunion and Fly-In gives new meaning to the expression "on a wing and a prayer."

Dawes Arboretum, Newark

DAWES ARBORETUM, NEWARK

MOUNDBUILDERS, NEWARK

Courthouse Christmas Lights, Newark

Ohio University, Athens

Y Bridge, Sunrise, Zanesville

If you've ever received a postcard displaying an aerial photograph of a rather odd looking "Y" bridge and the trademarked phrase "Turn Right in the Middle of the Bridge," then you've received your mailing from a visitor to Zanesville.

The only "Y" bridge in the world, this forked treasure boasts three ends where U.S. 40 — the old National Road — crosses the confluence of the Licking and Muskingum rivers. The structure, first built in 1814, is unique because — as *Ripley's Believe It or Not* accurately noted — it's the only place in the world where it's possible to cross the bridge and yet stay on the same side of the river.

The bridge, located in the center of town, is actually the fifth incarnation of the structure to be built on the same location. The noted Midwestern bridge-builder Carl Schumacher came to town to live during one of the bridge construction periods, contracted pneumonia and died — the bridge's only known fatality.

Zanesville, once the state capitol of Ohio in the early 1800s, is also known as the home of the Zane Grey Museum and as home to Roseville and Weller art pottery (the town's nickname is "Clay City"). Zane Grey, the famed author of paperback Western tales, grew up here.

Casey's Barbershop, Millersburg

Balloon Festival, Coshocton

Memorial Day, Somerset

Some have called the town of Somerset the most patriotic in Ohio — and with excellent reason. The tranquil village livens up every Memorial Day for a celebration that salutes, in part, Civil War general and heroic native son Gen. Philip Henry Sheridan. (Sheridan commanded the Union Army upon the retirement of Gen. William Tecumseh Sherman.)

The statue of Sheridan atop his bucking mount, in fact, is impossible to miss; the bronze giant was unveiled on November 2, 1905 in the heart of the town square. The event was covered by reporters from New York City to Washington, D.C., who described the enthusiasm of the townspeople as "being like the 4th of July in November." The dedication garnered such press attention, in part, because the monument — commissioned by Ohio's governor and state legislature — was the creation of noted New York sculptor Carl Heber.

The Sheridan Monument was delivered on a flatbed railroad car; 16 draft horses, supplied by local farmers, then tugged the massive bronze creation the half-mile from the railway depot to the village square. A nearby cannon was donated during World War II, during one of the many scrap drives held by Somerset's residents to support the war effort.

And, yes, the 4th of July is a pretty big deal around these parts, too.

John Glenn speech at the Statehouse, Columbus

JOHN GLENN SPEECH AT THE STATEHOUSE, COLUMBUS

STATEHOUSE, SKYLINE, COLUMBUS

57

Concert on the River, Columbus

58

CONCERT ON THE RIVER, COLUMBUS

SANTA MARIA, COLUMBUS

59

City Hall, Columbus

CITY HALL, COLUMBUS

Wexner Center, Columbus

WEXNER CENTER, COLUMBUS

Ohio State Fair, Columbus

Battelle Park, Columbus

Christmas Lights, Clifton

Journey to the tiny village of Clifton, near Yellow Springs, anytime during the month of December and you're sure to encounter the state's largest private Christmas illumination. Indeed, how could you miss it?

Clifton Mill, the largest operating gristmill in America, transforms its surrounding grounds and river gorge into a winter wonderland adorned in festive lights. Millions of lights. Legendary lights.

The mill's owner, Anthony Satariano, is certainly no dim bulb. After all, he's managed to turn a mere flour mill, miles off any beaten track, into an immense tourist destination that attracts 75,000 visitors each holiday season to the rural hamlet of Clifton (pop. 165). It takes six industrious individuals more than three months to string the 3.2 million bulbs.

You should plan to be there precisely at 6 p.m., when the lights are switched on in a single moment. To witness the mill, its 18-foot waterwheel and the surrounding snow-covered acreage convert instantly, from utter darkness into a magnificent array of light, is heart-pounding. The crowd of children actually utter a collective "whoosh."

Satariano also runs a virtual Santa Claus museum next to the mill, with more than 3,000 figures of St. Nick on display — all collected over a 30-year period. Many are mechanical and clockwork figures from long-shuttered Ohio department stores, which make for a nearly living, breathing North Pole experience.

"Just like Clifton, Santa Claus is timeless," observes the ebullient Mr. Satariano.

Air Force Museum, Dayton

The largest flight collection in the world. The oldest military aviation museum in the world. Ohio's most frequented free attraction.

These are just some of the descriptive lines used in reference to the United States Air Force Museum, located in the cradle of aviation itself: Dayton, birthplace of the Wright Brothers and home to the Dayton International Air Show.

The museum is located on the grounds of Wright-Patterson Air Force Base, in Area B, and showcases more than 200 airplanes and jets as well as assorted missiles and German V-2 rockets. From a World War I Sopwith Camel to a B-29 Super Fortress circa World War II, just about every significant moment in the history of flight is represented here, up to and including spacecraft such as an Apollo command module.

Perhaps most notable — and most eerie — is the hangar that displays every Air Force One since the days of President Eisenhower. As you move through the aisles of these presidential transports, you can feel as if you're moving through history itself, especially when you board the Air Force One that took President Kennedy on his fateful trip to Dallas.

Once you're done strolling the 10 acres worth of planes parked in a series of huge hangars, you can cool your heels watching a selection of large-format films about flight at the museum's IMAX Theater.

Sixth Street, Sunset, Cincinnati

HARRISON STATUE, ELM AND GARFIELD PLACE, CINCINNATI

Cincinnati Chamber Orchestra, Memorial Hall, Cincinnati

UNION TERMINAL, CINCINNATI

71

Cincinnati Ballet performance at the Contemporary Arts Center, Cincinnati

CINCINNATI BALLET PERFORMANCE AT THE CONTEMPORARY ARTS CENTER, CINCINNATI

Oktoberfest, Cincinnati

Roll out the barrel! Cincinnati's annual Oktoberfest — held, oddly enough, in September — just happens to be the largest Oktoberfest in the world after Munich's beer blast.

Tradition holds that some celebrity — Tony Orlando, Weird Al Yankovic and The Monkees' Davy Jones have done the honors in past years — lead the annual kazoo symphony and chicken dance. Tens of thousands of free kazoos are handed out, as each year the festival attempts to break the world record for largest chicken dance ever.

Oktoberfest attracts some 500,000 revelers, all nibbling edibles that include metts, bratwurst, sauerkraut balls, sausages, potato pancakes, Limburger cheese, cream puffs, strudel and other low-cal fare. Yes, quite a few brews are swigged as well. You can then try working off those "kalorien" by yodeling or doing the polka.

One unique local creation to sample is goetta, a German meat product (pronounced "get-uh") that's a combination of steel-cut pinhead oatmeal, pork, beef and seasonings.

Oompah! Even the music is authentic — bands imported straight from Bavaria. And if you're asking why Cincinnati has the planet's second largest Oktoberfest, here's the answer: The city is largely of German extraction, once boasting street signs in Teutonic languages.

Ohio State Marching Band, Paul Brown Stadium, Cincinnati

FLYING PIG MARATHON, CINCINNATI

Tall Stacks, Cincinnati

SUSPENSION BRIDGE, SUNSET, CINCINNATI

Reindog Parade, Mt Adams, Cincinnati

GOVERNOR BUSH CAMPAIGNS IN BLUE ASH, CINCINNATI

Holy Cross Immaculata Church, Cincinnati

82

HOLY CROSS IMMACULATA CHURCH, CINCINNATI

SWAIM PARK, CINCINNATI

83

Fireman's Festival Queens Contest, Laurelville

Head to the hills! The Hocking Hills, that is, that rustic region of Ohio known for its incredible landscapes and getaway resorts as well as such quaintly named attractions as Old Man's Cave and Tar Hollow.

Deep into western Hocking County, you'll encounter the village of Laurelville (pop. 490), a quaint pit stop where "the pace of life is slow," according to the hamlet's own semi-official motto. Located at the intersection of state routes 56 and 180, scenic Laurelville trades on its historic roots in the lumber industry. Today's shopkeepers barter wood crafts and old-fashioned hardware as well as produce from the local fruit orchards.

And, each July, there's the highlight of the Laurelville social calendar: the Fireman's Old Time Festival, started in 1923. You'll find down-home country cooking, the Fireman's fish fry and the Queen Pageant, where some lucky local teen is crowned queen for a day. "Visiting Queens" are past winners who return for the special ceremony on Saturday evening.

A traditional auction of prize cakes, baked by the ladies of the town, supports the volunteer fire department. (And lest you depart with the impression the auction is somehow penny ante, it raises more than $12,000 annually.) A tractor pull, baby beauty contest, big wheel race and grand parade round out this classic slice of Americana.

Mozart Festival, St Julie Billiart Church, Hamilton

Rt 93, Coalton

ROUTE 93, COALTON

Adena, Chillicothe

YOCTANGEE PARK, CHILLICOTHE

Car Show, McConnelsville

A small town doesn't necessarily equate to a small event. Take the Classic Car Cruise-In, which roars into McConnelsville in Morgan County every year and pumps 1,500 visitors into the local economy. Approximately 125 vehicles surround the town square and its immediate environs for the automobile show, now in its 18th year.

"We have anything from 1914 to the present," boasts organizer Walter Dalzell, who runs the Classic Car Cruise-In as a benefit fund-raiser for the M & M Jaycees. "There are classic cars, sports cars and other cars, all divided between modified and original and shown in divisions, divided by every 10 years."

The Classic Car Cruise-In is emceeded by a disc jockey who plays 1950s rock & roll tunes and other appropriate music to accompany the displays of antique vehicles, vintage coupes and restored trucks.

Photographer Tom Schiff says he just happened by the show and was amazed at the variety, from Model Ts to muscle cars. "I would say 95 percent of the cars were from close by, say within a 35-mile radius," he says. "Guys just sit around and talk about their carburetors."

Ash Cave, Hocking Hills, Logan

ASH CAVE, HOCKING HILLS, LOGAN

FRENCH PARK, GALLIPOLIS

Shoe Repair, Gallipolis

In downtown Gallipolis, residents have been sauntering into B & E Shoe Repair for the better part of three decades for a shine or sole fix. Bill Stapleton first opened B & E for business on January 1, 1970. The "B," of course, stood for Bill, and the "E" for his wife, Edith. Since those early days, son Steve Stapleton and John Clonch have joined the business.

The younger Stapleton notes that the moniker "shoe repair" probably doesn't do the shop justice. "We fix everything these days, if it's glued, riveted or sewed," he says. The Stapletons have taken on everything from gun holsters and leather coats to horse saddles and even trampolines.

And, of course, the traditional shoe buffing. "We charge $2.50 for a shine, but if you want to shine 'em yourself, you won't hurt my feelings. We have two chairs, but we don't do a lot of while-you-waits anymore. People are just too busy to wait, so they drop off a bag of shoes to pick up later.

"You can probably tell in the photograph that we're set in our ways. We don't have a computer. We don't have email. We just have a rotary phone and an old cash register."

Index of Photographs by City or Town

Akron
    Akron Aeros at Canal Park Stadium, 36
    English Garden, Stan Hywet Hall and Gardens, 35
    Soap Box Derby, 37

Athens, Ohio University, 49

Bowling Green, Wood County Courthouse, 16

Bucyrus, Music at the Mural, 20

Celina
    Amphicar Swim In, 8
    Mercer County Fair, 10

Chillicothe
    Adena, 88
    Yoctangee Park, 89

Cincinnati
    Cincinnati Ballet Performance at the
        Contemporary Arts Center, 72
    Cincinnati Chamber Orchestra, Memorial Hall, 70
    Flying Pig Marathon, 77
    Governor Bush Campaigns in Blue Ash, 81
    Great Hall, Cincinnati Art Museum, 73
    Harrison Statue, Elm and Garfield Place, 69
    Holy Cross Immaculata Church, 82
    Ohio State Marching Band, Paul Brown Stadium, 76
    Oktoberfest, 74
    Reindog Parade, Mount Adams, 80
    Sixth Street, Sunset, 68
    Suspension Bridge, Sunset, 79
    Swaim Park, 83
    Tall Stacks, 78
    Union Terminal, 71

Cleveland
    Church in Snow, 25
    The Flats, 30
    Hall of Fame and Science Center, 28
    Library, 32
    Public Square, Sunset, 27
    Severance Hall, 33
    Skyline, Sunrise, 26
    Westside Market, 31

Clifton, Christmas Lights, 64

Coalton, Route 93, 87

Columbus
    Battelle Park, 63
    City Hall, 60
    Concert on the River, 58
    John Glenn Speech at the Statehouse, 56
    Ohio State Fair, 62
    Santa Maria, 59
    Statehouse and Skyline, 57
    Wexner Center, 61

Columbus Grove, Swimming Pool, 12

Coshocton, Balloon Festival, 53

Dayton, Air Force Museum, 66

East Liverpool, Diamond Area, 42

Gallipolis
    French Park, 93
    Shoe Repair, 94

Hamilton, Mozart Festival, St. Julie Billiart Church, 86

Kirtland, Holden Arboretum, 34

Laurelville, Fireman's Festival Queens Contest, 84

Lisbon
    Steel Trolley Diner, 38
    Town Square, 40

Logan, Ash Cave, Hocking Hills, 92

Mansfield, Town Square, 22

McConnelsville, Car Show, 90

Milan, Melon Festival Parade, 23

Millersburg, Casey's Barbershop, 52

Mount Vernon
    Bicentennial Barn, cover
    Waco Airplane Reunion, 44

Newark
    Courthouse Christmas Lights, 48
    Dawes Arboretum, 46
    Moundbuilders, 47

Oberlin, Graduation, 24

Somerset, Memorial Day, 54

Tiffin, Uncle Mike's Ice Cream, 18

Toledo
    B-29 Cockpit, 15
    Glass City 200, Toledo Speedway, 14
    Toledo Art Museum, 13

Upper Sandusky, Grain Elevators, 19

Wapakoneta, Wapa Theatre, 11

Wooster, Air Force Band Concert, 43

Youngstown, Fellows Riverside Gardens, 41

Zanesville, Y Bridge, Sunrise, 50